The Things We Did, All the Things that We Do

poems by

Brian Burmeister

Finishing Line Press
Georgetown, Kentucky

The Things We Did, All the Things that We Do

*For the survivors
And everyone we have lost.*

*We owe it to them
To learn,
To speak,
To act.*

Copyright © 2019 by Brian Burmeister
ISBN 978-1-63534-843-9 First Edition
All rights reserved under International and Pan-American Copyright Conventions. No part of this book may be reproduced in any manner whatsoever without written permission from the publisher, except in the case of brief quotations embodied in critical articles and reviews.

ACKNOWLEDGMENTS

The following poems originally appeared, sometimes in slightly different form, in the following publications:

"Monument Circle" (as "Monument Circle, 2004") and "Exchange Rate (as "Discount") in *Social Justice Poetry*.
"Please Understand" (as "Fatima Cries") in *The Feminist Wire*.
"Garsila Village" in *The Camel Saloon*.
"Margins" in *Blue Hour Magazine*.
"Currency," "Confirming the Crime," and "Capturing What it Can" in *Bindweed Magazine*.
"Present Tense," "More," and "Paper Words" in *805 Lit + Art Journal*.
"Steps in Darfur" in *Yellow Chair Review*.
"Proof of Purchase" in *Red River Review*.
"Disconnect" and "Justice I." (as "Blockade") in *Verse Virtual*.
"Hate Begets" (as "Transmigration") in *Dual Coast Magazine*.
"Make Me What I'm Not" in *Eunoia Review*.
"Two Dollars" and "Darfur, as Seen from America, March 2009" (as "Darfur, March 2009") in *Right Hand Pointing*.

Publisher: Leah Maines
Editor: Christen Kincaid
Cover Art: Pietro Pazzi
Author Photo: Danielle Burmeister
Cover Design: Leah Huete

Printed in the USA on acid-free paper.
Order online: www.finishinglinepress.com
        also available on amazon.com

Author inquiries and mail orders:
Finishing Line Press
P. O. Box 1626
Georgetown, Kentucky 40324
U. S. A.

Table of Contents

We Concern Ourselves 1
Monument Circle 2
Please Understand 3
Garsila Village 4
Exchange Rate 5
Margins 6
Present Tense 7
Steps in Darfur 8
Proof of Purchase 9
Colors Are Brighter There 10
Disconnect 11
Hate Begets 13
Justice 14
A Reflection on Words 16
Currency 17
More 18
Make Me What I'm Not 20
Paper Words 22
Heresy 24
Elimination 25
Confirming the Crime 26
Two Dollars 27
Capturing What It Can 28
Darfur, as Seen from America, March 2009 29
Why We Look Away 31
Something, Somewhere 32

Beginning in 2003, the Sudanese government empowered a militia, the Janjaweed, to eradicate rebel armies. The Janjaweed's mission was savage. Unfathomable. They were also to remove—by any means necessary—the entire self-identifying African population of the country. Primarily centered in the Darfur region of western Sudan, this campaign of terror, violence, and genocide resulted in the displacement of millions, the tragic deaths of hundreds of thousands, and countless rapes—particularly among those women and girls who ventured from the internally-displaced-persons (IDP) camps to retrieve firewood.

Meanwhile, in The Democratic Republic of the Congo, decades of civil war ravaged their nation. As in Darfur, the death tolls were incalculable. A culture of rape as a spoil of war was rampant and rationalized by many of the soldiers involved in the conflicts.

The poems that follow are based on, inspired by, and sometimes include quotes from news articles, documentaries, and speeches detailing these tragedies.

All of the author's proceeds from this book will be donated to the World Food Programme, which did and continues to do great work assisting those living in these regions and in conflict-affected nations around the world.

WE CONCERN OURSELVES
(an IDP camp story)

Six boys kick
        The sandy brown ball back
            And then
      Back
Smile
        Then kick
            Back and then
      Back
Every day at the camp.

Twenty feet away, two girls
Sit,
      Watch,
           Stroke
The coarse fur of a teddy bear missing
Right arm,
      Right leg.

They smile, too.

And yet,
In classrooms everywhere,
      We concern ourselves with
           What
We can
      Teach children.

MONUMENT CIRCLE

12:03 p.m., in front of great stone
soldiers and sailors,
cars go round and round.

A dozen people stand
together, at the steps of the gray,
limestone tower, over a hundred years old.

Most of them hold white signs,
with simple block text:
PRAY FOR DARFUR 1 PM

A few cars honk or wave,
most passersby on foot pick up
their pace, drop heads.

At 12:04, one couple walks up,
in their sixties,
still holding hands,

asks a sunglassed college girl,
holding a sign,
"Who is Darfur?"

PLEASE UNDERSTAND

Fatima silently cries as she watches
    Her hair
        Fall to her feet.

Her father speaks slow as he watches
    His wife take the same straight blade
        To Fatima
    As she does to their sons.

Six years old, Fatima
    Does not
        Understand
Her father's words
    As he attempts to explain,
    "We must do what we can
    To keep evil away."
    Does not understand when he
    Approaches,
        Kneels,
            Kisses her hand,
    Whispers, "Someday, I promise,
        You will be pretty again."

GARSILA VILLAGE

In Garsila, there are
Brick walls scarred black without
Roofs, metal cauldrons
Surrounded by piles of ash.

Good or bad or unforgivable,
The things we make and do
Always outlive us.

In Garsila, there are
No sounds, no use
For any of this.

EXCHANGE RATE
(for Uganda)

When fathers exchange ten-year-old boys
To soldiers for promises

Of liberation, hope, and other words
That will only stay words,

Women become mothers without voices,
Whose minds, in time, won't

Be able to form the faces of their children.

MARGINS

The President scrawled, "Not on my watch,"
In the margins of a memo,
Then proceeded not to look.

We took his cue, did the same;
Our news pumped airwaves for months
With Anna Nicole,

While slow-motion devils
Rode horses with mechanized hate
Flying from their hands.

We pretended to complain.

I wrote letters, gave speeches,
Gave up. Turned
My tube back to Britney and Paris.

Sand and sorrow,
It seems,
Have nothing on blondes.

PRESENT TENSE

"It's like stepping through a time machine," He says, shakes his head. "Have you seen this?"
She sets their coffees down, Garfield ceramics steaming.
Morning reds flood the room.
"No." She takes the newspaper, sighs. His index finger tapping at the words. Her eyes scan, rescan. She says, "They have to use wood? Like camping?"
He nods, says, "There's nothing else."
"Every day? In order to survive?"
He says, "Keep reading."
She sits, keeps going.
He leaves to wake the children.

When he returns, she asks, "Why do the police do nothing?"
"They're part of the government."
He pulls two bowls from a cupboard, says, "They're all on the same team."
She folds the paper, stands. Kisses the children on their brows as they drudge in.
"So there's nothing for the women to do? That's it. Gather the wood and—"
"That's it," he says. "Simple. Either die in the camps from starvation or leave to get wood."
"But the things that happen to them out there."
"I know."
"It's terrible," she says. "So terrible. How can this happen?"

He pours Cookie Crisp into each bowl as she gets milk from the fridge.
The youngest says, "Mommy, what are you talking about?"
And smiling, she says, "Nothing."

STEPS IN DARFUR

When you walk barefoot here,

You'll notice the hardness of things,
Dried, harsh gray and ecru.

The ground looks like sand
But does not give.

Here, dirt, rock
Are the same.

Walking, running, the same,
Your feet do not sink.

In this place, not even knees get saved.

PROOF OF PURCHASE

A man far smarter than me
once said, "Show me your budget
and I'll show you what you value."

God, it seems,
might want the receipts,

might care the way we prioritize
Apple, Fendi, Wave Runner,
as if they were air, food, water.

Taking stock of one's life
means I confess I care more
about twelve additional inches of screen size
than saving a dozen families from malaria.

What reimbursement should I expect on that?

COLORS ARE BRIGHTER THERE

The women dress bright—
Canary, pink, emerald, scarlet—
Dresses flowing 'round legs,
Wrapped tight against face and torso—
Prints of flowers honor
That which no longer grows—
Stripes of darkness stand out against the light—
But it is that light you remember,
That canary, pink, emerald, scarlet—
Brightness, brightness—

DISCONNECT

He remembers:

His arm about her
As they sat on her crappy green couch,
The one her brother gave her
With the middle collapsed.

As they watched the film, she grew silent,
No words or nods for his comments.
The pixelated children before them, sleepless and hungry,
Confessed through the screen

That many of them saw
Their parents beaten or shot.

Or shot.

The hour grew long and her eyes
Never left the scrolling names of production workers

Until all was black.

He still remembers:

Thinking she must feel
A part of this world
He could not. That his heart
Was defective. Hers strong.

He could see the injustices and need
For things to be done. He, even he,
Knew his part, small, small, to write checks or letters
Or both.

And they sat, and they sat. Silent.

But he couldn't feel:

Those depths
Until two days later when she came over
For dinner and solved the mystery
By breaking things off.

HATE BEGETS

In Kalma they have Kalashnikovs,
Russian toys for African children.

The Dajo, Fur, and Zaghawa
Who died as one family

At the end of Janjaweed pangas and guns,
Now turn the worst kinds of metal

Against each other
In the name of peace.

Tribes who signed
The DPA, a pact for peace with Khartoum,

Have their homes burnt
In the camps, bullets lodged in their faces

By neighbors who think
Peace can only come through pain.

JUSTICE
(for all survivors)

I.

We went to the police
    To tell our stories,
        To see justice,
And the officers rocked their heads,
    Grinned.

They ripped our clothes,
We said.
    We explained they paraded us,
      Paraded us,
    In front of their men.

We told the police this,
    The awful *this*,
        Told all the things our mothers
Told us
    not to say.

The police, these men we told,
    Just nodded,
        Nodded.

                No questions.

They had small pads of paper
    In hand,
        Pens
        In hand,

    Yet the two never met.

When our stories ended, they simply nodded again,
        Smiled again.

"Thank you," puffed out of their mouths before they waved us away.
But do you know our names?

They placed their hands to our backs, pushed us away.
But do you know our names?

II.

Sara sat
        Under loud fluorescent lights
        Clutching her mother's hand.

The officer made his report.
"Name?" he asked.

She answered
        Question after question
As her mother sat silent. Still.

Down the hall, cheers
        And a mumbled television.
        Another homerun.

"Was there alcohol?"

"Did anyone see?"

"Are you certain it was him?"

Sara answered each as it came.
        Her mother voiceless beside her.

Later, she would remember
        His nod.
        His smile.

As she slowly absorbed the blame.

A REFLECTION ON WORDS

We
Abolish laws,
Annihilate atoms,
Delete characters,
Eliminate mistakes,
End stories,
Eradicate diseases,
Exterminate bugs,
Extinguish fires,
Obliterate monuments,
Purge stains,
Slaughter cattle,
Void coupons,
Waste time on words
As if they bring justice
To what happens to people.

CURRENCY

As children we're taught to love
our neighbors as we love ourselves.

But as our bones grow hard, we learn
to replace faith in love with fences—

our definitions shrink with age
until brotherhood is bound by borders.

The cries of Hutu and Fur sleep
in the dark blood of earth

      we pump in our cars.

The silence confirms
life is worth more in some places.

MORE

April 27, 2007

The camp crowds around radios:

The static, British voice tells
them that names have been
released
by the International Criminal Court.

Those gathered hold
each other, cry,
and await the list.

They say nothing for
fear they will miss
this *joy*.

And the promise of it comes:

"Ahmad Harun and Ali Kushayb have been . . ."

But there are no more.

The crowd
waits, waits.

And the promise is gone.

As the report continues for hours
it is clear that only
two names have been charged.

"Where is the devil Bashir? Where is his name?"

Voices raise, embraces release.
A small pot shatters as a young Sheikh walks away.

"How can there be only two?" someone asks
as the crowds go back to their tents.

The only reply anyone will remember, goes,
"There will be more.
        God will make there be more."

MAKE ME WHAT I'M NOT
(inspired by the heart and heroism of Brian Steidle)

Called forth by the last embers
And smoke,

Captain Steidle arrives at the village,
The sole American in the team of five.

He is hailed
By a small handful who survived

Because they were wise
To play dead.

A young, young woman
Brings her baby to him.

Captain Steidle is white,
Which must, *can only*, signify doctor.

      He is not.

The baby's back was pierced:
A bullet wound below the shoulder.

A second larger wound,
A mess of blood and skin

On the opposite side,
Just above the hip.

Captain Steidle speaks English to the woman,
She does not understand.

He removes his shirt,
Places it on the ground,

Takes the baby from her, gently,
Gently lays the child there.

He wipes away what blood he can,
Wraps the shirt tightly around the larger wound.

He shakes his head, whispers words,
But not to her, not to anyone near,

And asks for help.

PAPER WORDS
    On July 12, Sara wrote home to her parents:

In a different IDP camp, there was
    confusion. Word spread
That some were being moved.

    Which was true.

But the gossip was quick and panicked and
Evolving.

Within a day, there became great belief
That those being transferred
Were being taken to Europe.

When the cars and jeeps pulled into their line,
Mothers swarmed the vehicles
With their children,
Holding them out,
    Thrusting them out,
    And where windows were open,
        Throwing them through the space
    Between metal and glass
Chanting,

    "Take my baby, take my baby."

It took two or three hours that day
    For the children to be returned
    And for all that were there to know no one,
        Not one,
Was going to Europe.
Just twenty miles further west,
To someplace no better,
    Save for better supplies.

Each week Sara wrote to her parents like this:

Of the things she heard,
And not what she saw.

As if the two steps of separation
From parents to action
Would allow them to place her into the role
  Of story-teller,
    Not daughter.

HERESY
(inspired by the brave women in Darfur Now)

Can God forgive
us for what we do here,
in the sand, *this sin?*

The tree we cut is perfect, holy,
alone. It is wrong.
Janjaweed are in the jungle,

So we must come here—
they make us
come to the desert.

Make us steal impossible life.
They make us and
make us.

This heresy is theirs, God,
understand that.

ELIMINATION

"They're kicking us out," the director announced
    upon his entrance to the tent.
He paced and paced,
    kept repeating the same loud words.

They stopped sorting supplies.
No one could move, just stare.
    He marched and steamed,
until Sara asked,
    "What are you saying?"

His whole body shook,
    he couldn't calm down.
        "They're making us leave.
        All of us.
        Immediately."

"To a different camp?"

"Out of the country," he corrected.
    "Us. Everyone.
        Every camp everywhere."
    Punched his hands together, swore.

Each set of eyes shot to another's,
    as if someone's gaze might hold an answer
or a cure.

After a moment, Sara said, "They can't do that.
    We're here to help.
Don't they know we're here to help?"

And no one said a thing,
    or could even breathe,
    after he replied,

"It's done."

CONFIRMING THE CRIME

Friday morning in March,
    Six years into the crisis,
The floor of the U.N. assembly
    Floods and fills with alliteration:

Callous and calculated…
Significant signs…
Facing fear…
And Confirming the crime…

The careful selection of syllables
    Hopes to impress
Like a sixteen-year-old
    On a date, or in class.

But both date and teacher
    See through the sounds,
Know that beneath them
    Is something short
       of *real.*

In response, tragically true and confident words come:

"*The decision of the government*
of Sudan is a legitimate

sovereign decision

which
we
will
never
reverse,

and this should not be an issue for discussion."

TWO DOLLARS
> *(inspired by the dedicated law enforcement in*
> *The Greatest Silence)*

Dark shades propped to her forehead,
Sauda pulls a beige folder
from the cabinet behind her desk.

She is a tall woman with strong arms.
The only woman officer in the city of Kolwezi.
The only officer assigned to rape.

She crosses her small, yellowed office,
sits, slides a picture of a group of soldiers
to the white man,
uniformed in brighter white,
before her at the other side of her cluttered desk.

Sauda taps above a specific man,
a smiling man,
head cocked back,
gun in both hands before him,
instead of slung over shoulder like the rest.

She tells the man in white this man was in jail.
Was.
"But for two dollars they set him free."

The white officer stares, stares,
through the paper,
through the paper,
shakes his head.
He asks if the man is back at it.

Sauda reaches across the table,
snatches the picture back, says,
"We try to do justice.
This is fantasy.
Impossible.
So this world must change.
We must make it."

CAPTURING WHAT IT CAN

The too big, camouflaged uniform,
The small blanket,
> Wrapped, tucked, twisted
> About face and neck
To protect from bugs, heat, sun.

This is the first photo she takes.

A gun strap hangs over his right shoulder.
A red baseball caps sits loosely
> Atop the blanket on his head.

Following the photo,
He says to the woman, white,
> Surrounded by local officials, U.N. observers,

The camera capturing what it can of his wide-smiling face:

"You know how things are in combat zones."

The journalist asks of him what they do to women,
Why they do what they do to women.
Her interpreter speaks for some time.

The soldier shakes his head, laughs,
Laughs, shoves the question away with his hands,

"We have an antidote,
> *roots we take from the bush.*

When we take that medicine,
> *We cannot get AIDS."*

DARFUR, AS SEEN FROM AMERICA, MARCH 2009

James couldn't find it.

    He thumbed
        frantically
        furiously
            through the pages of *Newsweek*,
  but there was
      no mention
  of what his daughter
      had said on the phone.

So he was sure he had missed it.

He went back
    and read
        and reread every word in the table of contents.

    There was nothing of:
        Bashir.
        The ICC.
        The harrowing fact
        that 13 major non-governmental aid organizations
        were forced to leave the country
        as retaliation for the court's decision.

    Instead:
        He found a page devoted to
        "The Ugly Truth about that Poor Little Rich's Girl's Blog."

Two days later, Sara calls from Paris, before coming home.
    "This moment is so incredible," she says,
    "and tragic. Without doubt tragic.
        But ultimately wonderful.
    This is the moment, I know it.
    Everyone I work with in the camps,
    we feel that it is.

> *The breaking point.*
> Obama will respond.
> I just know that this has to end soon."

James says nothing of the magazines.

Nothing of the nothing he sees on the news.

Just, "I miss you." And more truth: "I want you home so, so much."

WHY WE LOOK AWAY

Perhaps it's a problem of scale.

Too big, too much, too scary
      Makes it hard to grab hold.

Far easier to look away
      to something else,
           Smaller,
           Familiar.

Nothing wrong with little things.

Except the highs they give.
      Just enough.

Never enough.

SOMETHING, SOMEWHERE
(inspired by Invisible Children)

The children study, sleep,
Five hundred of them,
Bags on dirt,
Ninety minutes from home
By foot.

Their march is what keeps them
From being soldiers.

Those left behind,
Rebels take,
Turn boys into murderers,
Girls into the worst kind of slave.

So they leave,
And return and
Leave and return,
Summoned, summoned,
By something, somewhere
Inside them
That says stay alive.

Though cracked and cold,
Bus-station concrete
So far from home
Is comfort,
Promise
Of something, somewhere.

NOTES

"Margins" quotes a phrase President George W. Bush is famously attributed as having handwritten on a report about the Rwanda genocide.

"Proof of Purchase" quotes a phrase often spoken by Vice President Joe Biden.

The title "Hate Begets" is borrowed from the famous quote "Hate begets hate" by Dr. Martin Luther King, Jr. This poem was inspired by *The Guardian* article "Violence Flares in Darfur's Kalma Refugee Camp as a New Cycle of Persecution Begins" by Jonathan Steele.

"Justice I.," "Two Dollars," and "Capturing What it Can," are based on, directly inspired by, and/or contain language and quotes from the documentary film *The Greatest Silence: Rape in the Congo* directed by Lisa F. Jackson, whose courage and compassion make this a better world. "Justice I." is loosely inspired by content and themes in the film. The title "Two Dollars" is borrowed from words spoken in the film and quoted in the poem, and the poem is inspired by the film. "Capturing What it Can" is directly inspired by the film and contains direct quotes.

The opening lines of "Currency" reference the lesson of Mark 12:31 in *The Holy Bible*.

"More," "Paper Words," and "Heresy," are based on, directly inspired by, and/or contain quotes from interviews in the documentary film *Darfur Now* directed by Theodore Braun. "More" is inspired by content in the film, and April 27, 2007 was the exact date the referenced charges were made by the International Criminal Court. "Paper Words" was inspired by the film and contains a direct quote. "Heresy" was directly inspired by the film and the italicized words are language used in the film.

"Make Me What I'm Not" was directly inspired by Brian Steidle. The poem is based upon a story told during his July 27, 2005 presentation to the United States Holocaust Memorial Museum. More on his life, activism, and the horrors he witnessed in Darfur can be found in the book *The Devil Came on Horseback: Bearing Witness to the Genocide in Darfur* by Brian

Steidle and Gretchen Steidle Wallace and in the documentary film *The Devil Came on Horseback,* directed by Ricki Stern and Anne Sundberg.

"Confirming the Crime" is based on and directly inspired by the *Reuters* article "Sudan Says to Never Reverse Decision to Expel NGOs" by Louis Charbonneau. The quote which ends the poem are the words of Mohamed Yousif Ibrahim Abdelmannan, as quoted in the article.

A sample of the lack of news coverage mentioned in "Darfur, as Seen from America, March 2009" can be found in the March 9, 2009 issue of *Newsweek*. The poem names an article from this issue.

"Something, Somewhere" was inspired by content in the documentary film *Invisible Children* directed by Jason Russell, Bobby Bailey, and Laren Poole.